Sat

Written by
Daisy Hawkins

Illustrated by
Andy Hamilton

Published in 2026 by
Norwood House Press
2544 Clinton Street
Buffalo, NY 14224

Printed in the United States of America

Library of Congress\Cataloging-in-Publication Data:
Names: Hawkins, Daisy, author. | Rickard, Stephen, 1957-, author. | Hamilton, Andy, illustrator. | Sotirovski, Aleskandar, illustrator.
Title: Sat / by Daisy Hawkins, illustrated by Andy Hamilton. Pat sat / written by Stephen Rickard, illustrated by Aleskandar Sotirovski.
Description: Buffalo, NY : Norwood House Press, 2026. | Series: Phonics all-stars: phase 2 |
Identifiers: ISBN 9781978577725 (pbk.) | ISBN 9781978577732 (library bound) | ISBN 9781978577749 (ebook)
Subjects: LCSH: Reading–Phonetic method–Juvenile literature. | English language–Phonetics–Juvenile literature. | Sitting position–Juvenile literature.
Classification: LCC LB1573.3 H395 2026 | DDC 372.465–dc23

CPSIA compliance information: Batch #CW26NHP: For further information contact Norwood House Press at 1-800-237-9932.

Sat.

Sat.

Sat.

Sat.

Sat.

Sat.

Sat.

Pat Sat

Written by
Stephen Rickard

Illustrated by
Aleksandar Sotirovski

Pat.

Tap,
Tap.

Pat sat.

Tap,
Tap.

Pat sat.

Pat sat.